SPEAK UP, SPEAK OUT... SHOUT IF YOU HAVE TO! (2ND EDITION)

Let Your Voice Be Heard

By
Random Thought, P.H.D

Rennell Parker, LLC
PO Box 2193
Florissant, MO 63032
www.rennellparker.com
Phone: 1-314-536-4899

© 2011 Rennell Parker. All Rights Reserved

No part of this book may be reproduced, stored in a retrieval system, or transmitted by any means without the written permission of the author.

Dedication

First, I must thank God Almighty for blessing me with an opportunity to follow my dream and let my voice be heard around the world. To my parents, brothers, sisters, family and friends thank you for your unconditional love and continued support over the years as my thoughts have traveled just as fast as time. To my wife and children, thank you for standing by me and understanding that the sacrifices we have made were not made in vain. And to all of you that have shown support for my various events and now for my first publication. I thank you and I love you all.
God bless.

PREFACE

Speak Up, Speak Out...Shout if you have to! Is the slogan that Rennell Parker created as means to educate, motivate, and inspire others not only in the United States, but throughout the world. Within these pages are not only words but they are experiences, dreams, obstacles... and testimonies of triumph.

Thinking back to the first time I heard the phrase, Speak Up, was when my mother would gently lift my chin explaining to me the importance of letting my voice be heard. While at the same time molding me into the man I am today. Along my journey I have been blessed to encounter obstacles that tested my manhood, my sanity, and more importantly my faith that has caused me to Speak Out.

What I do is not about me but about those that are destined to lead us into tomorrow. There are times when we speak and we still can not be heard...at that moment I suggest you shout if you have to! Poetry is life and Life is Poetry, so step outside your box, claim your victory as Random Thought has done poetically...**Speak Up, Speak Out...Shout if you have to!**

Phase I: Speak Up

...The Lone Sailor...
...Down Payment...
...Untitled...
...Criss-Crossed Conscious...
...Dance of a Melody...
...Deeper Than Eyes...
...Gorgeous...
...Love Storm...
...I Can't Breathe...
...Cupids Little Secret...
...Subconscious Love...
...You Have It...
...Rib of Me...
...Flame of My Fire...
...I Remember...
...Innocent Kiss...
...Love Hurts...
...Love Me or Leave Me...
...Calm Waters...
...A Glimpse of Loneliness...
...Untitled II...
...In Love with My Skin Part I...
...Comfort of Your Flesh...
...That Walk...
...ING...
...Ecstasy...
...I Surrender...

Phase II: Speak Out

...Real Men...
...Black for a Day...
...Wake Up Call...
...An Old Friend...
...Sleeping with My Thoughts...
...Fatal Fertilization...
...My Story...
...Honestly...
...My Life...
...Soul Invasion...
...Soul, the Soul Invader...
...United We Stand...
...Discrimination...
...United by Disaster...
...My Expression of Depression...
...I Don't...
...My Life Has Been Changed...
...Live a Little...
...By the Blessing of God...
...I Know...
...Death Becomes Her...
...Gone To a Better Place...
...Right on Time...
...Still Breath...
...The Living Dead...
...Between Friends...

Phase III: Shout If You Have To!

…Tomorrow…
…Reality of a Dream…
…Too Tight…
…Mother Earth…
…In Love with My Skin Part II…
…About the Children…
…Kate & Jake…
…Innocent Faces…
…Secrets of the Wind…
…Student of Life…
…Random Thoughts…
…Just Thoughts…
…Closing Walls...
…Check Out Time…
…Welcome to My World…
…Eternity…
…Thugged Out…
…Craziness…
…I Am…
…Rate…
…Not My Name…
…Name Me a Hurricane…
…Elevation…
…More Than a Random Thought…
…What is My Name?...
…Give Me Freedom…

...Continue the Dream...
...I Cry for My People...
...Sounds of the Village...
...The Negro Speaking of Rivers...
...State of Emergency...
...My Last Breath...
...My Last Poem...

Phase One: Speak Up

To **"Speak up"**;

1. Is to express one's opinion and feelings openly and without fear or hesitation at a volume that encourages understanding.

2. To speak loud enough to be audible.

3. To act as spokesperson.

The Lone Sailor

Several years and many months have passed, and the "Lone Sailor", has not yet begun to enjoy life in the military. Yes, he works hard and does his job with a smile. But in reality he is miserable. To anyone else his Soul would be so heavy that is it almost unbearable. But his spirit is unbreakable. Months and Months has passed since he has become part of the "Real Navy", yet he still wishes he was a civilian living a life full of mischief and weed smoking.

Now all he does is drink to the foam. Drink to the foam is what is sung in Anchor's Aweigh, but they want to label him an alcoholic, well, he is not, he just likes to drink a lot. I am the "Lone Sailor" and it is now that my voice will be heard. My heart will beat fiercely and my Soul will be relieved. Although I may be limited physically…the mind of a write is limitless and each thought lives without boundaries. I am the Lone Sailor… Welcome to My World…It is now that I shall SPEAK UP!

Down Payment

Take my heart as down payment for your love,
Take my mind as down payment for your thoughts,
Take my flesh as down payment for your touch,
Take my eyes as down payment for your sight,

Take my lips as down payment for your kiss,
Take my ears as down payment for your words,
Take my lungs as down payment for your breath,
Take my tongue as down payment for your speech,

Take my nose as down payment for your scent,
Take my spirit as down payment for your Soul,
Take my mind, my body, and my Soul as my final payment, for your hand and everlasting love.

Untitled

I often day dream of a sign to help me understand
my life,
And all of the options resulting in choices that lay
ahead of me,
Thinking about which path will I take, what move
will I make?
What is the difference between fiction and fake?

Is there a difference, am I once again,
Approaching insanity, is humanity too,
Overwhelming for me, I show love to so many,
But who really loves me,

Or is it the other way around, are they,
Loving me too much, and am I not giving,
Enough...If I can't trust myself,
Then who can I trust,
How can I control these feelings of lust?

Criss-Crossed Conscious

My thoughts:

"Every morning, I awake in confusion, who is this woman kissing me, what is this illusion. What has caused this emotional intrusion, I have never felt anything as real as the way our lips mesh together by way of fusion, and frozen with sweat as our bodies groove to the beat of sex drums, my eyes amazed by the coke bottle shaped lover as she pours her love all over me, I can't help but to drink from thee, the humming birds now humming to me,

Foreshadowing an emotional climax and she is no longer touching me, but physically just the way she looks at me, and how I can imagine her love feeding and fulfilling me, completing me. But I don't understand why every morning I rise I feel the same feeling and her face is not on the woman lying next to me."

Her thoughts:

"Every moment I spend with him is wonderful. The way he looks at me and speaks to me, although his tongue by itself speaks a mouthful. To be in his arms is so delightful. And he always treats me with the utmost respect, as if I were a true Queen. I just don't know how to dissect what this truly means. What does he really desire of me? Is he just treating me to have his way with me sexually? If so, I better put it on him right, so I can keep him next to me, and help take care of me.

He has trapped me just the way he stares at me with thirst in his eyes as if he is suffering from oral dehydration and the taste of me is the only thing to satisfy him while his manhood tries to dance closer and closer to me. And every morning I have the opportunity to lay with him as he looks at me as if it was his very first time witnessing the image of me."

Dance of a Melody

Feel the beat, hear the music, become the melody,
I'll be the lead all you have to do is follow me,
You move so gracefully, now it is you that I am following,

As my eyes become amazed by the delicacy of your entirety,
On this floor we are linked by the Soul, dancing and sharing everything, Still living the life of a melody, in my heart this image shall never leave,

Whenever my heart beats a beat, my mind visions you and,
My feet begin to move rhythmically, my Soul has never felt such sensitivity the thought of you has conquered and taken over me,
Your touch, equivalent to the sensation of ecstasy,

I desire for your love to drug me, I love the way you dance,
I love the way you hug me, you groove my mind away from my troubled history,
I will be forever in a trance, after becoming one with you and dancing the…Dance of a Melody.

Deeper Than Eyes

Walk in my shoes, choose what I choose,
Win what I lose, use what I use,
Visualize the colors of my blues and you'll see,
My Soul is deeper than eyes can see,

See what I see, be who I be,
Feel my pain, and you'll see, still I'm not free,
My Soul is deeper than eyes can see,

Show what I show, learn what I know,
Follow where I go, flow as I flow, you'll see,
My Soul is deeper than eyes can see,

Say as I say, play as I play,
Kneel to the ground and pray as I pray, you'll see,
My Soul is deeper than eyes can see,

With your eyes view what I view, do as I do,
Do you understand me, do you, can you? You'll see,
My Soul is deeper than eyes can see,

Be as clear as the skies, as dirty as lies, louder than heaven's cry,
As hypnotized as the art of surprise, you'll see,
My Soul is deeper than eyes can see,

Now think as I think, Say what I think,
Do as I think, look deeper than my eyes, and you'll
see,
My Soul is deeper than eyes can see.

Gorgeous

Sophisticated lady perfect to a "T",
Beauty so bright she blinds your sight to see,
She prances with elegance,
Gorgeous…

But never with arrogance, but confidence,
Her style intense, her smile carries you to suspense,
But you can't rinse,
Gorgeous…

Out of mind, she's a 12 she surpasses a dime every time,
With her classiness, her sexiness with no stress,
She's the best dressed from head to toe, and back to breast,
She can be nothing less than,
Gorgeous…

She's got deep dark eyes and sexy shaped thighs,
Delicious lips and a magic Queen-Dom between her hips,

She's Gorgeous…
She's Gorgeous…

And she's got ass, she's got class,

But you can't have her unless you've got that emotional finance,
You have to give her romance or you don't have a chance,
To hold those Gorgeous hands.

Love Storm

Rain, thunder, you light me,
Clouds, Skies, you cover me,
Storms show how we love we,
My heart giving off vibes of vibracity,
Within your eyes is security,

Within your arms, all of me,
Within your thighs is ecstasy,
The rain now cumin' within we,
Love Storm, Reality or Fantasy?

Can't Breathe

I miss your touch, I miss your voice, I just miss you
so much
I can't breathe without you

All I can do is hope, because without you I can't cope
I can't breathe without you

You scent is gone; my heart won't work because I'm
so alone
I can't breathe without you

Now my tears shall, all I crave is you, just you that's
all
I can't breathe without you

My lungs are feeling tight; in my mind there you
stood all of the night
I can't breathe without you

Like an egg missing from a nest, there is a whole
within my chest
I can't breathe without you

For our love is a celebration, and if it ends, begins my
suffocation
I can't breathe without you.

Cupids Little Secret

Cupids little secret,
He's a sneaky little devil,
He would follow behind me going where ever I would travel.
Traveling for work or personal matters,
Together he brought us and nothing else mattered.

Cupids little secret,
He's a sneaky little devil,
He followed her around so her love to me she would unravel,
Cupids little secret, was a map of unplanned love,
Love for me and love for her,

In reality that is as real as the breath that we breathe,
Because of cupids little secret, we both cry when it's time to leave.

Subconscious Love

Dancing on the stages of my eye lids was a woman with beautiful skin, sparkling eyes, and the body of a Goddess, but with the walk, of a Queen.

As I sit in the audience of my mind, I find myself day dreaming of conservations with myself asking is her skin soft, what color are her eyes, and what does it feel like to be enclosed within the warmth of a Goddess?

Without the make-up, without the stage lights, without the stage, who is this love that has captivated the subconscious state of me? As I became witness to the gracefulness of her movement, I began to fantasize of her touch, her scent, her voice.

My Soul now bowing to the groove-ment of this Goddess sent Queen. My eyes smile at her smile, and my applause for finale has no ending. For it is the confidence in her walk, the imagination I have of her speech, and the desire to feel her touch is what brings me to my feet.

As she exits the stage, she approaches me, and before she can say a word, I tell her, I am honored to have witness the dance of an angel. Then the lights flickered and just like an angel she disappeared, then I awoke, realizing I have seen my destiny, I have witnessed the dance of my Subconscious Love…

You Have It

I don't know what it is, but you have it,
It's in your smile, it's in your walk, and it's in our eyes,
What you have I crave it,
I crave your style, your talk, and the love beyond your thighs,
You posses a mind as free as the clouds of the skies,

You are my "MU.DA.PO[1]."
You are the MUsic in my mind,
You are the spirit embracing my Soul with your DAnce,
You are the POetic inspiration in my thoughts flowing towards my hands,

I don't know what it is but you have it, You have it on the tip of your lips, You motivate my Soul to grow with the love of your kiss and the womb of your hips, You are the Goddess of the Moon with the hypnotizing glow, Baby… you are the love that I have grown to know,

You have the strands of hair worn by my Queen,

---

[1] MU.DA.PO. – stands for Music, Dance, and Poetry

You have the left-handed ring finger fit for my
diamond-cut ring,
You have the only love fit for this king,
I know what it is, and I have strong desires to claim
it,
You are the Queen, therefore, you be the judge of me,
I stand before you on trial to endure what you have,
because you have it.

Rib of Me

With each breath, my lungs expand making me breathe easy, thoughts of you coming to see me, my Soul enriched with solid gold living a fantasy, soon you will provide me with memories, I have desires to show you magical, passionate sceneries, we believe because we both know we believe we, you can sense it inside of me, you breathe the breath I am breathing,

I feel the pain you are grieving, together we dance the rhythm our heart is beating, it's you and only you , there is no such thing as cheating, no love leasing, I can't see myself falling and being caught by no other being, I am willing to give you all of me, in due time I will be giving you an engagement ring, yet we must take things slowly,

We both know timing is everything, and at the right time our love shall make us both sing, what you ask you shall receive, I desire to give you everything, all that I have mentally, all that I have emotionally, all that I possess spiritually you can have, proving I am you and you are the rib of me.

Flame of My Fire

The flame of my fire is my Queen,
She is the drive of my desire and keeper of my dreams,
She is my Queen from the sun to the wick her dance begins to groove gracefully,

Rocking to the rhythm of the wind,
My Soul feels her heat as my heart sways to her beat,
Her love creates a spark setting fire to the sheets,
She is the flame of my fire melting my flesh like wax,
The essence of our movement is stroking my entirety,
The rhythm of the flame allowing me to relax and reach my physically sanity, Luring me away from reality manipulating my Soul to turn to a land of ecstasy,

Creating my own fantasy by burning brighter than the light of day,
Screaming louder than the words I say,
Reflecting the answers to the prayers I pray,
She is the orange, blue, and red rainbow of my life,

The Flame of my fire dancing bright and bold,
The way she warms my atmosphere assures I'll never be cold,
Love can't be sold,

Yet if her glow was for hire, I would be the buyer,
She is the, Flame of my fire.

I Remember

I remember all of the joy; I can still feel the pleasure,
Your smile, your touch, your kiss, and your thoughts,
I still treasure.
Which I thought to be, "Deeper than eyes can see",
At that time I wasn't for you, and I remember
someone saying you weren't for me,

We shared each other in so many ways,
Still to this day my heart wonders, trapped in a maze,
My Soul lowered then raised, yet I still give you the
intimate praise,

Alerting myself that you were the best,
So that I may be careful of the memories that
enhance my stress,
You were number one, nothing less, your name
tattooed beneath the flesh
Of my chest,

Because I remember how you touched me internally,
You left me in a way that made my heart stop
bleeding, pumping and working fine, yet beating but
not bleeding,

I remember how most of the pain was caused by my
own ways,

The way I thought, the way I acted, like cause and effect,
When some thing happened, how I reacted,
The secrets, the deception even though I felt I hid nothing,

You went for the interception, just like cause and effect the reaction
Was my eruption, because your assumption was an interruption,
Starting temporary destruction, I fell in love with you and your spiritual seduction,

So to say that someone is seducing me better
Is like saying between H20 and water, H20 is wetter,
It just doesn't make sense, so rinse the thought of cheating,

Get that out of your mind; take time out and think,
In the mean while give me some time,
Don't pressure me and we'll be fine, when we made love, you felt my heart, my Soul, and My Mind…
Do you remember?

Innocent Kiss

You are so funny, so beautiful, so smart,
You are the first person to ever control my heart,
When I see your wonderful face and incredible eyes,
My whole body shakes and then my spirits start to rise,

You gave me a gift more valuable than sex,
Time is of the essence, so I cursed my Rolex,
You came into heart with your smile so bright,
No longer my choice, I fell in love that night,

I am going to miss the softness of your lips,
Dreams of missing the stimulating swiveling of your hips,
You could be my soul-mate and my true love,
Every night I'm on my knees, thanking the lord above,

Calling your name and seeing your face,
Are just a couple things that I will miss…
Most of all I will miss hugging you and receiving your
Innocent kiss.

Love Hurts

Internal pain, shockwaves thru the brain,
Blood turning blue in the veins, head banging like trains,
On railroad tracks, because of the hurt brought upon by the deceiving facts,

Blacks killing blacks, men in slacks, and women in skirts,
Conversations consisting of deceiving flirts,
But there's a thin line in one's mind when it comes to love, lust, and time, causing chills up the spine,
because one may be lost in time trying to find,

What is behind the greatness of the light?
And gives us the sight to see,
Just think how could my love hurt me?

Love me or Leave Me

I can hear your thoughts; I am the one to blame,
I have realized my faults, don't point any fingers,
Do not call any names, for I am ashamed of my actions,

I have pushed you to the left and off to the side.
Love me or leave me, tell me you love or by yourself you will ride,

I told you either, or, but you chose both,
You chose to love and lift me high, then you left leaving me low and dry,
Tears in my eye because you didn't say good-bye…

Calm Waters

As the Lone Sailor sits in solitude, waiting patiently to be in the arms of his love's desire. Watching the sunset all alone with laughter all around him, the skies are clear and the winds are whistling heavenly tunes as his source of light transfers from the sun to the moon.

Now he waits in darkness, as his Soul follows the "North Star" to freedom... freedom; freedom is what he craves, freedom to love, instead of being sworn to this ship as if he is some medium-wage-paid slave,

Dreaming of love and all of its benefits, he receives comfort from the dancing stars that appear on the stage of Calm Waters with the image of his true loves innocent kiss, his heart delivers the beat as his Soul begins to dance with this.

A Glimpse of Loneliness

Staring into the computer screen, typing words of sadness having thoughts of being elsewhere, but no one cares about my unhappiness. As I continue to stare I am listening to the soulful sound of Luther, wishing I had my love sitting beside me telling me how much she loves me. But I can only settle for emails and the imagination of her voice.

There is no simulation for her touch. As my son grows and understands more, I have envisioned him turning to his mother and saying, "Why isn't Daddy here no more?" I don't know how much more I can take before I break. I am emotionally, physically, and spiritually hurting.

My tears dance as they flow from my heart to my eyes. I have an illness that can only be cured by the loves of my life, I need my son, I need my daughter, and I need my wife.

Untitled II

Your eyes have trapped me, as beautiful as can be,
Your smile enlightens me,
I desire to be wrapped within your entirety,
All I see is we sharing our destiny,
Fulfilling each other's fantasies,

As I became you and you became me,
10/25 represents our anniversary and the day we said
"I Do"
This poem has no title…
Because there isn't a title that can capture the love I have for you.

In Love with My Skin: Part I

I am in love with me…
I am in love with my skin
I am in love with me,
I … AM…In... Love…With…

The skin that we live in,
Your skin, his skin, her skin,
Baby, you know I love your skin
So in love, that from within my skin
He created the rib of me,
God did it so easily
Lord I thank thee. Amen

Comfort of Your Flesh

Receiving pleasure to the third degree,
Your flesh becoming me,
I am the flesh understudy of your fantasy,
The virtue of your reality,
The "X" in your land of ecstasy,
I am the Soul your flesh is comforting.

Your flesh casts away the pains of my stress,
The love of your flesh fitting my manhood proving
your love is the very best,
Creating soothing grooves within the womb of my
chest,
Secretly in your flesh is the hiding of my flesh,
Our Souls become whole within no added stress we
are one and shall be nothing less,
Proving there is no greater treasure than the comfort
of your flesh.

That Walk

Created to perfection, she's the resurrection of
Beauty,
Her lips, her face, her hips, her waist, her booty,
From her eyes to her thighs, she's got the juice
She creates a boost of confidence because…That
Walk…is so intense…

Blurred visions, cloudy foggy thoughts, clear sight,
Pure sexiness inside her mind displaying reflections
of brilliance
Thru the stroll of her stride,
Dynamic sensations spread throughout by the glow
of her pride…
…That Walk…

The suspense of my mind enhances…That Walk…
Which performs a sign of positivity thru the
productivity of…That Walk…

On a horizon of wondrous lands she's got my mind
in her hands
And my heart in her eyes like an innocent angel
using,
…That Walk…
To hypnotize those who despise the art of surprise
because……That Walk…

Produces my Soul to rise…
…That Walk…
…That Walk…
…That Walk…

<u>ING</u>

Beginning…
Talking…
Dating…
Hugging…
Kissing…
Loving…
Proposing…
Engaging…
Marrying…
Babying…
Growing…
Learning…
Living…
Dying…
Everlasting…

Ecstasy

Influenced by a prophecy
Power of a vibrant sensation
A meaningful journey that's meant to me
Dreams worlds of great creations

Starring into the core of wondrous lands
Traveling when there is no day nor is there night
Touching its beautiful surface not knowing its plans
Visions seen, yet not with the normal sight

Beginning to feel what you imagine
A gentle move, a soothing groove
Visualizing what is soon to happen
Loving its surface for it feels so smooth

Breathing unknown, unsteady, and weird
Pumping fluids of essentiality
Ecstasy, worlds of magic with nothing feared
Breathing is slowed by words of confidentiality

The voyage will soon come to a halt
Ecstasy, with sacred quarters to relax
Filled with memories stored in a secret vault
A journey waiting to reach a climax

A climax comes at the very top

Rushing quickly through what are now shaky lands
It comes as a feeling that can't be stopped
Rumbling through the deepest sands

For Ecstasy is a place of enchanted love
Started by two Souls who are perfectly matched
Exotically placed from mystical powers above
From the spirituality of the power another climax has hatched

A calm breeze slowly sets in
Positioning itself with fearless ease
Where did this Ecstasy begin
Ecstasy, I want you to last forever… Please

Music so sweet, words not spoken
Ecstasy, a world of art
Asleep in a dream never woken
The mind of a pure creative heart

Some think the end is near
This is only the beginning
Emancipate yourself from here
Ecstasy; a world of story never ending.

<u>I Surrender</u>

Shifting sands, Waving Seas
A Lover's touch, like a gentle breeze

The sun smiles, as the wind whispers
While the Trees dance, to the tune… of a million whistlers

Telling a story, Folklores of Nature
Soundtracks of love, composed by our Creator

Loving deep with passion… so sweet, so tender
I give in to it all… for your love; I Surrender

Phase II: Speak Out

1. To **"Speak Out"** is to talk freely and fearlessly, as about a public issue or a private issue publicly.
2. Issues ranging from Race, Depression, and Life after Death

Real Men

Real men don't cry, we may rant and rave, and pace back and forth, but for what it's worth... real men don't cry.

No matter what we are going through, we are determined to remain hard as a rock, and not even the giant atop Jack's beanstalk, could squeeze water from the rock. There is no pain too great that we can't handle, there is nothing that we can't figure out, because we know it all, we got all, and that is all we need, more liquor, more weed, more silliness adding to our insignificant greed. Insignificant is our greed for power, our greed for money, and our greed for sex. But because of that greed we have neglected what we desire, what we need. And until we are able to awake, our Souls shall never be freed from the treachery of greed. That is how we remain hard as a rock, not even the giant atop Jack's beanstalk, could squeeze water from the rock because...

Real men don't cry, we may rant and rave, and pace back and forth, but for what it's worth... real men don't cry.

It takes a real man to say "I Do", it takes a real man to have a choice, and think before he elects to choose.

Various choices stand before him, yet he shuns the decisions that bore him, and take on the opportunities that challenge him. Because a real man looks forward to a great challenge as a chance to prove to those that surround him that he is the man they think he is. Some believe that it is the challenge that makes the man; a man. And not the Man that makes the challenge. A man has to come to terms with himself, to separate want from desire, in order to make the "right" choice for that man, to determine what is and what is not a challenge. It takes a real man to have a choice, and think before he elects to choose. As there will be various choices that stand before him, yet he will shun the decisions that bore him and take on the opportunities that challenge him because…

Real men don't cry, we may rant and rave, and pace back and forth, but for what it's worth… real men don't cry.
A real man says "I DO" to start and be a mainstay for his family. Whether he says "I DO" at the alter or says, although we are not together, I "DESIRE" to do all I can for my child and "I DO" believe although we are not living in the same house we can still work together to raise our child the best way we can, "Together". A real man eliminates the word "greed" from his vocabulary and counts his blessings

for having his needs fulfilled and being able to achieve what he desires; and learns to want for nothing. Because...

Real men don't cry, we may rant and rave, and pace back and forth, but for what it's worth... real men don't cry.

I am a real man by every sense of the phrase. I have eliminated greed from my vocabulary. I have deciphered the difference between want and desire.
I am a real man, and I cried when my parents purchased my first car. I have cried as lives have come and gone along my journey of this thing called life. I have cried in pain. I have cried in mourning. I cried when I said, "I DO". I cried when my son was born. I cried when my daughter was born. I am a real man by every sense of the phrase. As I traveled the path known as my living, growing from a boy to the man I am today, I have cried many times along the way. And yet I remain a "Real Man", solid as a rock, by every sense of the phrase. Yet some believe real men don't cry, they may rant and rave, and pace back and forth, but for what it's worth real men don't cry.

So tell me, because of my tears of pain, my tears of struggle, my tears of relief, my tears of success and

my tears of joy, does that make me any less of a man?
No…..,
I am a man, A Real Man by every sense of the phrase.

Black for a Day

Live in my skin,
Comb thru my hair,
Smile with my grin,
Live my life and you tell me what's fair,

Face the hardships a black man faces,
Feel the pain I feel,
Go to court, count the black faces,
Imagine silver metal on your beautiful brown skin,
Now that's the real deal,
Realism providing painful facts,
For just one day try to be black,

Inherit the beauty of our Negro minds,
The sexual greatness of my Nubian Queens,
The divine strength of our black backs and spines,
Have the gold of our Soul to purchase all things,

Purchase freedom with my mind, love with my heart,
All things created from darkness,
"Light" is just a spark,
A spark of unconditional love,

Which in one day; from above came a mystery of life,
Without the carving of a knife, God created my
caretakers,

Larry and Jenay, A strong black man and his
beautiful black wife,
Realism providing beautiful facts,
For just one day try to be black,

Can you handle all that?

Wake-Up Call

My eyes are closed, I'm so very tired… man I'm beat,
Now I'm tossing and turning still sound asleep,
Trying to get up, but they are holding me down,
Let me go, get off me… set me free,

I am lost and confused,
I feel trapped and all alone,
And my wounds are starting to bruise,
I feel like I only work to lessen the pain,

Life as I knew it, is over
Father, why do they beat me?
Why do they hate me?
Why do they fight me until I call him master?

"Wake-up "N-Word"
You are having a bad dream,
Brother, slavery has been over with."
If it has ended why do you use that word?
Why do I feel this way?
Brothers and Sisters,
We need a Wake-Up Call.

An Old Friend

I woke up early because I am going to meet an old friend today. We use to be best friends, but we lost touch along the way. Where ever he went I would follow along and play. Whatever words I would speak, he would kneel with me and pray. Always saying whatever I would say,

I am getting dressed early, because I am gong to meet with an old friend soon. Whatever I would wear, he would wear it too. We would stand "face-to-face" and say, "Boy you look good, well I'll be damn, look at you…" Incase you didn't know whatever he would do, I would too,

I am reuniting with my best friend today, because I am tired of being alone. I smell good I'm looking fresh, and feeling very strong. I would never be where I am today, if he hadn't been the spine within backbone,

I am going to meet an old friend today and my heart is beating fine. He is flesh of my flesh, you know a true friend of mine. With similar thoughts, we even have the same frame of mind. Our meeting is right on time,

I am about to speak with my best friend, we shall converse alone, with no one else. This conversation clearer than most, we whispered to each other you have to come close. We looked deep into the mirror and conversed with thy-self. "Hello my friend, you are me and I am you, we can be no one else".

Sleepy Thoughts

Anger, hostility, having nightmares of viewing myself as others may see me, engaging in conversations with myself, fighting and arguing about sanity,
I could care less about humanity,
I will forever be in secrecy,
Even though through my thoughts there is no hiding me.

You must search deep and intensely to find me,
When I am sleeping you can't wake me, not even if you shake me, No woman can break me, Those who may be ignorant are hating me, They don't know…that…don't nothing phase me,

On the trial in the back of my mind is the issue of insanity, I try to live my life honestly,
Everything I do is not always because of me,
There is another living and breathing inside of me,
And when I am alone the thoughts I am sleeping with,
Begin to frighten me.

Fatal Fertilization

Lying words, and false impressions of love making, unjustifiable sex and deep penetration can be breath taking, Intense stares and bone-chilling words are the cause of the divine Soul shaking,

Virginity taking imitating, fatal fertilizing, loving deep, causing irregular patterns of sleep with the holder, Creating 9 months of carrying a boulder of love filled with intensity. What made it a fatality was my stubbornness and nothing could fulfill me,

I let the truth elude me, I tried to escape my destiny but that's hard for me when in reality I felt as dead as can be. Yet no one has killed me, I lost my mental identity,
I felt death run through me,

Lord knows that I enjoyed the unification of bumping flesh,
Becoming one, creating one, now a year later after the first creation,
I am taking full responsibility for that Fatal Fertilization,
Experiencing real love, while trying to lead a fake life, I apologize to my son, I apologize to my wife.

My Story

I was a child acting wild, playing around with the pleasures of life,
Taking jokes serious and neglecting reality,
Moved away from home at age 19 not yet grown,
No education, no work, as I desired to live alone,

I had no money trying to pimp and slang some love meat just to make ends meat,
Messed around and got dumped so I was all alone in the dark doing a praise dance asking the Lord to help me, While living the life of a dead beat,

My stress almost killed me, it was sort of ironic because my depression kind of saved me,
Smoking that "green", bathing, and sipping on coca-cola mixed with Hennessey,
I began to glare in the mirror singing to an image with 2 of me,
As my words say, "AS I look at you, I see 2 of me, enjoy yourself. It's time for me to leave."

After being down so low who could have foreseen a speedy recovery,
No matter how hard I tried something always added to my misery,

There was nothing any one else could do, I was the
only one that could please me,
So I rolled a blunt and again sipped on my
Hennessey…
At that point I was happy!
Then I realized my happiness was Killing Me.

Honestly

Honestly, honesty eludes me the fears I have often
fear me, the love I crave sort of destroys me,
I feel like an endangered species,
Drenched in rain that fell beyond the trees,

Water level beneath my knees but I'm drowning,
With very slow breathing, my baby could be teething,
But instead I cause grieving and fears of me leaving,
360 degree spinning, the desire to do away with
sinning, After "Death" left me alive spinning,

My heart grinning, because I now have a new
beginning, A "Book" to read in,
From Genesis to Revelations, I can smile again,
My life didn't start until I had approached my end.

My Life

My life, how and where do I begin?
In the beginning or middle, because only God knows the end,
There have been times when I was joyful and happy,
There were days that he could have given up and forsaken me,

I have felt love as well as rejection,
I almost got hit by a car and died at an intersection,
There are people I love and also love me,
There is no greater love than the love for my family,
My Life…

My life has had its share of ups and downs,
My life has had its share of smiles and frowns,
I have made it through my crushes and infatuations,
I have also made it through the toughest situations,
Judgment Day is coming and I am not afraid,
Cause I will be marching up Zion in Jesus' parade,
I have had family and friend's who have died,
And through each passing I have smiled and then cried,
My Life…

I have been blessed by God since beyond the age of seven,

Through my goodwill and faith when I die I'll walk up that stairway to heaven,
I have had many sleepless days and sleepless nights,
But Mama always said,
"Believe in him and pray and everything's going to be alright",

I have done everything, but I haven't done it all,
I have admitted my sin and now patiently awaiting God's call,
Throughout my life some things could not be understood,
But with God on my side everything is all good,
My Life.

Soul Invasion

Love's guard erosion created by a hearts explosion causing corrosion of the mind and the lack-ability to find what is behind the force penetrating ones mind,

Strolling up the incline plane of the spine to the brain using its power to drain what remains the same after the alteration of the change, yet with minimum range which may feel strange intellectually, mentally, spiritually, and emotionally,

Making love an unconditional, sensational, traditional feeling of wrong doing, choices of choosing, winning and losing, feelings of perception and bad interpretation,

Traveling thru the environment with no hesitation bringing factors of influence with love being their insurance to insure the protection and safety of the flesh from head to toe, back to breast, and reducing physical stress,

With a break thru causing unbearable pain in ones chest meaning there are limitations to the quality of protection because there is no such thing as perfection, as their mind and flesh was crossed and left at the intersection of love and lust, lost trust because it's a must to dust the walls of intrusion before the illusions of ill intent and a misleading imagination causes internal displeasures by an unwanted Soul's Invasion.

The Soul Invader

I am Soul, the Soul Invader, the elevator of the mind, the manipulator of time; I am the MU.DA.PO, spirit of rhyme,
I am Soul, the Soul Invader, The leader of the paper chaser, the suspect of the Soul taker, the love of the love maker; I am Soul, the Soul Invader,

I invade thru the iris of your eyes, I soar thru your body as clouds of the skies, thru you I grow stronger, then exit thru the gland of your cries, I am Soul, the Soul Invader, the changer of what was taught, the stranger of your thoughts, the danger of your faults, I am Soul, the Soul Invader,

I am the dance of your vision, the sounds of nature when you choose to listen, I am the glow your life is missing, I am Soul, the Soul Invader, I am the attitude caused by stress, the internal skeleton withstanding the pressure of your flesh,

I am the artist conducting the harmony within your chest, I am Soul, the Soul Invader, I am the image in your mind, the joy and stress of your cries, the dark and the light of your eyes, I am the thought your mind can not rinse, I am Soul, the Soul Invader…

I arrive through your dreams then leave you in suspense.

United We Stand

"I pledge allegiance to the Flag of the United States of America", but what do we pledge when no flag is standing there, People dying, Terrorist proving they don't care, about death because of how much they don't care about death, what makes you think they care about us, they don't give a damn, if we fuss and fight, our people killing our people, and now United We Stand.

Holding hands, while everyone is attempting to get right with the holy man. Too late, because war is the plan, Earth sinking deeper in the a universe of quick sand, beneath the land of what we call greatness, more like a place trying to withstand destruction, craziness, and unmanliness as we chant United We Stand!

Discrimination

The world is full of hate, discrimination is his name,
There are blacks hating blacks, blacks hating whites,
whites hating blacks, hatred towards women in
slacks, whites hating whites,
Is there no one who can see the light?

Muslims hating Christianity, this whole world has
reached insanity,
There is hate in the workplace, and why, because of
someone's weight, religion, or their race,
When will it all be erased?
Why do people stare when they see interracial dating
and biracial children?

The whole world has gone crazy.
They look straight pass the beauty of a person's
character
Judging them by their exterior features,
Looking at minorities as if they were creatures,
Who labeled the minorities a minority?
It can only be the teacher.

United By Disaster

United by disaster, help provided all over the world,
But who's helping us?
Who have offered to give us helping hand?
Our own country saddened with sorrow, but what are we doing to help?
Are our tears genuine?

Tears formed within my heart because there are children without food, wearing filthy clothing, they have no shelter and no family,
Resulting in a feeling of no love creating volcanoes sized voids of depression,
I am willing to open my home for those who need help,
I am willing to feed the hungry and love those whose only need is love.

Expression of Depression

I spoke with the bottle, and I asked him to drink with me,
As I walked to my garden; telling him to smoke with me,
Looking in the mirror saying, brothers please pass me the Hennessey,
As the mirror stared back at me,

I clinched my fist and began fighting with the imagery,
Causing a bloody mess in an attempt to destroy myself,
Seeing nothing to live for, having nothing to cry for,
Mentally playing a game of hide-n-go seek with Sanity,
At the time I really didn't care about you or me, I just didn't care anymore.

I robbed myself and told me,
I have nothing, you might as well kill me, stab me, shoot,
Do as you will just don't let nobody find me…Anomie…

Mentally and emotionally sentence me to four walls of freedom,

Candles all around sort of resembling my burial,
My Soul watching over all whom are at my funeral,
Crying, rejoicing, and grieving over the loss of me,

My spirit was so deep in thought that in a lonely state of mind,
One glare in the mirror and I would envision an image of three of me,
Me sitting besides myself,
And I… Begin to add on stress appearing to myself as if I am happy,
Yet the mirror told the truth, I needed sleep,
But I was too depressed to rest.

I Don't

You mad at me
I get on your nerves
You think I don't care…
I don't

You keep calling me lazy
You say I'm a bum
You think I don't care…
I don't

"Why are you like that?"
Those are the words people say
You think I don't care…
I don't

All I do is hoop
You don't think I care about you
You think I don't care…
I don't

I have no feelings
I show no emotions
You think I don't care…
I don't

You say I'm stubborn

You say I'm mean
You think I don't care…
I don't

I am not afraid to die
But you are
You think I don't care…
I don't

Everyone says I'm nice
But you think I'm cruel
You think I don't care…
I don't

You think I don't care about you
You think I don't care about me
You think I don't care…
I don't,

I DON'T… SO QUIT ASKING!

My Life Has Been Changed

Giving thanks for my blessings everyday,
Respecting others and the words they say,
Living and dying for my family in everyway,
My life has been changed…

No more hazardous smoking and drinking,
I react to every reaction by thinking,
No fear, face to face with adversity no more blinking,
My life has been changed…

Natural high, no need for drug and alcohol stimulation,
My wife, our life no more senseless fornication,
A loving husband and passionate father, my eternal occupation,
My life has been changed…

On one breath our Souls took flight,
Trading life for love and love for life,
My Soul combined as one with my wife,
My life has been changed…

Together as one soaring thru the skies,

The twinkling, shine of a little star in her eyes,
My wife, my child our life on a rise,
My life has been changed…

My life is different now,
I have a wife now,
I am a father now,
My life has been changed…

I'm only 21; I am growing up fast,
Excited with each day, having a blast,
I love my wife, till the end we'll last,
My life has been changed…

I now have adult responsibility,
I shall develop authority through sensitivity,
I can now display my fatherly ability,
My life has been changed…
My wife, full of life and compassion,
Our life, a future full of joy, pure satisfaction,
Our child, the circle of life, Gods Chain reaction,
My life has been changed…

Since 1981, my life has been arranged,
Chasity Lynette Parker, never did sound strange,
Till death do us part, as one we'll grace the stage,
As of, 25 Oct 2002, for the best,
My life has been changed.

Live a Little

Live a little, open your eyes then open your mind to distinguish the difference between hurtful cries and painful lies that penetrates your Soul thru your eyes but don't be surprised if your Soul cries because of your own lies as you visualize these cries don't become hypnotized but realize you have got to live a little…

To live a little you have to care a little, you have to care to live, while some people live to give instead of receive others are growing as victims to their own selfishness and greed. Want for nothing because God shall give you what you need. Live a little and pray, then what you ask you shall receive…You have got to live a little…

Live a little, live to grow, grow to know, know that you can grow to be whatever you can visualize and see. Speak Up, Speak Out… Shout if you have to, say, "No one can be greater than me." As long as you know you have to live to grow.
Live a Little.

The Blessing of GOD

By the blessing of GOD, anything is possible,
By the blessing of GOD, everything is capable,

By the blessing of GOD, we may attain eternal life,
By the blessing of GOD, we may meet our husband or wife,

By the blessing of GOD, we must have faith and continue to pray, By the blessing of GOD, when we are in trouble with us, He will stay,

By the blessing of GOD some things may not be understood,
And in times of hurt and pain, by the blessing of GOD,
Everything will be all-good.

I Know

I know the highest power,
To thee I give all the glory,
Listen to the story,
And praise his name.

I am a witness to his power,
I am a servant under his word,
I sing praise unto him in the shower,
God is my guide, God gives me strength,
Wherever I need to go, God is my ride; God is who I'm with,
When God speaks nothing else is heard. God is the creator and above all things,
Emanuel, God is with you and God is with me.

I know the highest power,
To thee I give all the glory,
Listen to the story,
And praise his name.

My will is nothing without the things God has done,
My fate would be unreal if Jesus was not his son,
I may have clothes; perhaps I would have home cooked meals,
But what is a home with no Soul, if I had a "Friend" named Satan and together we made a deal,

A deal on the issue of eternity,
Life before death and damnation after humanity,
With eternal flames chosen over happy days,
equivalent to that of insanity,
Satan providing unbearable brutality,
My faith in God assures I shall never fall subject to
Lucifer's mentality,
If you look in my eyes you'll see who's backing me,
The devil's clan will forever be terrified, with God on
my side there is no stopping me,
All because…

I know the highest power,
To thee I give all the glory,
Listen to the story,
And praise his name.

Death Becomes Her

Death becomes her as she searches for something never lost,
Unstableness grows because she feels that she is paying for something that has no cost;
So she bows her head and prays for God to deliver unto her what she thinks is lost,

Death becomes her, while at this moment of silence,
Her heart can't dispense the pain of someone she misses,
And she feels his love as the wind blows,
Because what she feels is the touch of his kisses,

Death becomes her as she remembers his voice,
She remembers his smile even though understands God's choice,
She wishes he would have stayed a while,

Death becomes her as tears race down the face of the Angel-hearted Queen,
Enhancing the beauty of a tombstone,
Her heart pounding and her head aching because of the pain of feeling alone,

Death becomes her as she grieves for not having him near,
Then her breathing grows cold and slow as the wind whispers to the tune of his voice with pressure, applied upon her chest saying, "Here, I will forever be here."

Gone To a Better Place

Gone to a better place, no more suffering, no more pain, Gone to a better place no more snow, no more rain, Gone to a better place we love her, and she loves us,

Gone to a better place to be with God's Son, Jesus, Gone to a better place, living happy days for eternity, Gone to a better place, smiling watching over you and me, Gone to a better place in heaven, so far apart, Gone to a better place, away from us, but in our heart,

Gone to a better place, a loving Sister, Aunt, and Mother, Gone to a better place, is not just anyone, She's our Grandmother, Gone to a better place, this is far away from the end, Gone to a better place, everyone smile her life is about to begin,

Gone to a better place, all of the hurt is completely through, Gone to a better place, Birdie L. Parker our Grandmother, We Love You!

Dedicated to Pastor Birdie L. Parker (July 9, 1927 – June 13, 1998)

Right on Time

It is hard to discuss someone you love,
When they are spiritually resting with the Lord above,
God came Right on time.
It's hard to cope when they're not around,
Family, hold your tears, don't cry when this body is laid beneath the ground,
God came Right on time.

Life may seem strange when he's not physically near,
Everyone put your hand on your heart because he lives in here,
God came Right on time.
What else can we say it's hard to explain,
The name Gary Sandford, forever planted in our brain,
God came Right on time.

When one of us is on the court and a voice magically appears,
"Shoot the ball" that's my Uncle Gary whispering in our ears,
God came Right on time.
He started to suffer but always stayed strong,
He lived his life to the fullest as if nothing was wrong,

God came Right on time.

From your nieces and nephews whose lives you have touched,
Uncle Gary we love, and we miss you so, so, so much,
God came Right on time.
There isn't a moment that our heart beats and you're not on our mind,
We may think you left too soon, but we know God came Right on Time.

In loving memory of Gary E. Sandford
July 3, 1949 – November 13, 1999

Still Breath

Strolling with darkness upon an unknown terrain,
Nervous with stiffness from my feet to my brain,

I heard unsteady breathing; something's coming near me, So I started running; something was trying to get me,

I'm not stopping I've got to keep going, as I talked to myself, Then I began to see outlines of familiar objects in chalk, Realizing I can see no one else, I just see myself.

The Living Dead

Walk amongst the living dead,
Endure the pain that lives in my head,
Make it big and share my dreams,
Is it pleasure or pain, what does this mean?

My body is fine, not a scratch nor flaw,
Life in shambles, accidents cars hitting cars,
Breaking hearts but never any bone,
I am living a nightmare, yet I got a "Love Jones",

Sentenced to the entrapment of water,
At times I may mistake my crying for laughter,
Jack fell down and broke his crown,
But Jill did not come tumbling after,

Now my mind is in a mental block,
Now the insanity of my words may stop.

Between Friends

Between friends, can I tell you something, because I have a secret? I am coming to you in confusion I hope you get it. I'm lost and hurting; you can feel my pain thru my touch, see my misery thru my eyes, and fear within my voice. Between friends I have to tell you, I have no choice.

My secret lies deep within, I feel the hair prancing upon my skin, this is only hidden behind my grin, just confide in me, you'll be by my side till the end, provide me with signs that you understand the pain in my mind. Dance with the beat of my heart, when you start, please show visuals of your dancing art.

Between friends, can I tell you something, because I have a secret? I am coming to you in confusion I hope you get it. I'm lost and hurting; you can feel my pain thru my touch, see my misery thru my eyes, and fear within my voice. Between friends I have to tell you, I have no choice.

I have to tell you that I am opaque in a colorful world, I am grooming into a man amongst women, boys, and girls. I cry to you from the stall of this room, between friends I have to tell you soon. I have had dreams of being a professional ball player, I have had nightmares of being taken away by ghost appearing, "Nigger-Slayers", I have a secret, I hope you get it.

Between friends, can I tell you something, because I have a secret? I am coming to you in confusion I hope you get it. I'm lost and hurting; you can feel my pain thru my touch, see my misery thru my eyes, and fear within my voice. Between friends I have to tell you, I have no choice.

I have secret meetings, different greetings, because I have confusing feelings. I have encountered a special Soul on this journey of life, she has something special, you know, something special like a wife, something I can't explain in words, you know the thoughts in my mind, the ones you've heard, she is my dream keeper, my humming bird.

Between friends, can I tell you something, because I have a secret? I am coming to you in confusion I hope you get it. I'm lost and hurting; you can feel my pain thru my touch, see my misery thru my eyes, and fear within my voice. Between friends I have to tell you, I have no choice.

She is my laughter, she's in my cry, she's in my smile, she's in my eyes, she's in the work of art reflecting my heart. She's in my flesh, she's in my bones, she's in my dreams, she's in my home, she makes me whole, She is my Soul. As her Soul flows free, she becomes my body, she becomes my Chi. Between friends, God, I thank you for knowing my secrets and for the direction in which you have guided me.

Between friends, you know my fears, why I shed tears, you have shown me signs that you ease the thoughts within my mind, Between Friends, you have been the light beyond my sight, you are that bright Star smiling over my prayers at night. From Random Thought to Ren, thank you for my voice. Between Friends, Lord I am your servant, this is my choice.

Phase III: Shout If You Have To!

1. If you decide to **Speak Up** and you have not been heard, then you must **Speak Out**.

2. If you have Spoken Out, and they still can not hear your voice…Then **Shout if you have to…**
   Let your voice be heard!

   Listen to my voice as I shout from within

Tomorrow

As I awakened with the sunrise
I thought of yesterday stressed with regret
Clinching my dreams, full of tears and sweat
Tossing and Turning, it took forever to open my eyes
Thanking my Creator, as I awakened with the sunrise

I thought of yesterday stressed with regret
Going through my day with a mind full of sorrow
Well, today is better than yesterday, maybe, just maybe I'll have a better tomorrow
With my head held high, I can wipe away my stress
No longer thinking of yesterday stressed with regret

Going through my day with a mind full of sorrow
With replayed images of an unforgiving past
Listening to others first, hearing my own voice last
Peer pressures of joy, now my happiness you can borrow
Save a life to change a life
No more minds full of Sorrow.

Reality of a Dream

There are many different clouds, yet they are all the same as they live in harmony amongst the skies,
My brother, my sister we must open our eyes
To realize that all that we have shines on us from beyond the skies,
Yes we are all different, but yet we are all the same within God's eyes,

He dreamt a dream with all the colors of the rainbow,
He dreamt a dream where man of all nationalities could travel to wherever it is that they desired to go,
With no limitations, totally free, believing that you can be you, and I could be me,
The key word is free, free from physical captivity,
Emancipated from mental and emotional insecurities,

No more raping our Queens. No more killing our Kings,
Allow our children to grow with each other,
Encouraging them that they can be anything,
We must show them the pathway to the Reality of a Dream.

Too Tight

From death to love and love to living,
Be thankful for what you receive and the art of giving,
Breathe before dying and stress before resting,
Life before strife and black before white,
That's right there was darkness before there was light,
My life has been wrapped Too Tight.

Mother Earth

I open my eyes and I see the heavens above me resting as the clouds dance across the river of Jordan, The Kings and Queens bathe and baptize their offspring in the river of Euphrates,

While the river of the Nile struts her stuff across the heart of the homeland with a rhythmic dance ever so elegant and prideful, Her grace was silent as without a word she spoke a mouthful,
Her beauty incredible, her love unconditional, her spirit travels all over from here to there, from Egypt to Israel,

Swimming along the Ivory Coast down to the capes of South Africa across the Atlantic to South America as part of one continent, her touch is soothing like the sand dancing across the Sahara hand in hand with her significant other, Father-Time, on a beautiful beach in Madagascar,

From dirt we become her children and it doesn't matter where we are… because she is never far, not even,
If we traveled far – far away on… what some call banana boats, or even slave ships,

Leaving home always has its benefits, we will forever be lifted and our Soul spirited as we dream of competing in Greek Olympics over Mount Olympus as in Greek Mythology, We are living in an aging economy, Life after life, species to species from death to birth;
I love "Our" Mother, Mother Earth.

In Love with My Skin: Part II

Finally emancipated from my mental slavery,
Filled with the Holy Spirit, through with living this life
Dangerously,

In the past more in love with sin,
Than I was with the temple in which my Soul temporarily resides in,
The insanity of the world is killing me,
Killing our minds, killing our dreams, killing our children,

Erasing the innocence of those innocent faces,
At 4 & 1 my kids can read sentences, Education;
Changing my major to Mathematics from Communications,
So that they can understand the numbers within the census,
6 young men sentenced to death for school fights and juvenile business,
Death meaning mental evaporation,

FREE JENA 6!!!!! FREE JENA 6!!! FREE JENA 6!!!

OH! Those precious black faces,
Speak up, Speak Out... Shout if you have to...
Let your voice be heard to unite as 1 across the world,
Supported by soldiers and sailors defending our nation tomorrow will be our boys and girls,

I know, because my job was to purchase the bomb the pilot dropped on Fallujah while they were praying,
In Love with my skin...The Time is Now!
In... Love... with my skin...The Time is Now!
In... Love... with... my... skin...The Time is Now!
Do you hear what I'm saying?

Teach love not war to our children,
I am in love with my skin,
Loving this handsome chocolate skin... My skin...
Listen, Listen, Just Shut up and Listen!!!!!!!!!!!!!

Mr. No love & Ms. No Motivation,
See I love her lemon drop, caramel top, and her chocolate addiction,
You see I'm in love with the skin of my Queen more than me, this fact not fiction, my benediction,

Sisters, please forgive me for my language and my actions,
I just want all to understand me,

No matter your complexion, in your mirror is God's Reflection,

In love with my Skin, Alpha and Omega,
Beginning and End,
The only thing I love more is God, and the skin worn by God's Children…
Now say it with me… I am in love with my skin.
I am in love with my skin...
I Am in Love With My Skin...

About the Children

Close your eyes open your heart and listen,
Take time out to think about the children,
Think about their smiles and laughter,
Think about building not breaking their character,

Let them know they are smart and they are loved,
Teach to them the powers of our Lord above,
Explain to them the consequences of doing right and wrong,
Encouraging words helps them keep their head up and always stay strong,

Stay near to guide them upon the correct path,
Insightful words shall prevent them from challenging God's Wrath,
Let them know they too can in their own way part the Red Sea,
Teach them about Emanuel hear them say, "God lives in me",

They are not kids, but young people,
Instruct now while they're young or their growing will have no sequel,
So whenever you are about to act a fool, take a minute and listen,

Call a timeout for yourself and think how your actions may affect our children.

Kate & Jake

I'm a speaking beast, a storytelling messenger, pounding my chest in the name of love from hip-hop to the tip-top of the highest mountain, soul gliding across the widest seas, With thoughts deeper than the deepest valley with anointed visions of raising dry bones up from that valley, doing spin moves on the opposition tossing alley-oops to the next generation, promoting love back into our existence…

Because in our community love is what has been missing, the reason for hating, domestic violence, and love's dismissing, the down fall of communication causing babies to be raising babies due to premature ejaculation & false impressions of LOVE MAKING…
They are ignorant of love and know nothing about what they were making,

Calling procreation a mistake and… abusing the babies they make and… asking for a break for Christ sake… but for Christ sake Jake should've thought about that before he laid down with Kate and Kate before she laid down with Jake…knowing that they fell in and out of hate… because love was never there, she was intoxicated by his words high off of the sound of "baby I love you"… never realizing he never cared

Now he's a daddy, confused, and unhappy…having a baby with a lady that thought she was his baby… realizing she abused him just a he abused her using her hips and waist to manipulate his money and get her way thinking it's funny, now she's his baby's mommy… instead of making love they made hate and now it's too late to take back his sperm the baby is 8…

So when we do the math it's 105 months too late and every 365 it's another birthday… so the question is what do we do now, How do we manifest a dream from a society with a plagued concept of fate, when will Love overcome the crippling affect of hate?

Innocent Faces

Faces so sweet, hearts so pure,
Minds not made, thoughts unsure,

No problems to be solved, nor choices to be made,
Just use six inch voices, no bills to be paid,

No troubles, no work, no stress no worries,
Christmas-Santa, Easter-Bunny, Tooth and Fairies,

They have innocence to the 3rd degree,
Trapped on earth, but their minds completely free,

Taught evil as a result of their teacher's ignorance,
Shivery dying, learning the art of arrogance,

They have a need for love to fill their hearts spaces,
How could one ruin the life and minds of these
Innocent Faces?

Secrets of the Wind

Sssshhh!... Listen to the secrets of the wind, stories of your grin,
And how you breathe over and over again,
Listen for the wind to enlighten you of your sin,
Free your mind to inherit the Secrets of the wind,

Sssshhh!... Feel the Secrets of the Wind grazing your flesh,
The wind stroking the interior of your chest,
The wind calming your stress,
Sway with the rhythm of the winds to soar above the rest,
Why is not a question, so if you test the wind beware of nature's wrath,

Sssshhh!... Travel with the wind like air dwellers of the skies, Allowing the breeze to be your tour guide in the skies, Witness the beauty and wonders of watching the sun rise,
Visualize the Secrets of the Wind,
The skies will not be the limit but you will have no limit beyond the skies,

Sssshhh!... Within the voice of the wind you will hear Soul pleasing words,
To the rest of the world you grow deaf,

Hearing nothing else, maturing, growing, and
learning while breathing on "One Breath",
The Secrets of the wind can only be found in oneself.
Meditation.

Student of Life

I am a student of life, trying to make it through all of life's adversities, with every breath trying to deal with humanity,
I refuse to lose my sanity because of someone trying to abuse or degrade me, it is my destiny to achieve greatness, I can do anything.

I don't need any one to support me or even aid me, God has my back, and the brightness of His light shall be my guide and lead me, into the reality of my fantasy, while my body is motionless, yet my mind is elevating smoothly,

As my Soul dances across the thoughts of my entirety,
Flowing freely beyond this atmosphere of controversy,
Paralyzing pressures of pleasure like having an orgasm while being under the influence of ecstasy, learning lessons from each situation,
With no hesitation teaching to others what has been instilled in me.

Random Thoughts

Consistent images of words,
Performing real time songs of now and old,
Dancing nouns, and singing verbs,
Subconsciously performing acts of stories told.
Each vision fighting with the other,
Like the bickering of aching Thoughts,
My brain erupts like a volcano
My head splits resembling a quake along the San Andreas Fault.
Swallowing my mind, devouring my Sanity,
These words don't even come close to representing the Random Thoughts that live within me.

Just Thoughts

Rivers flowing with tears of fears and pain internal,
Chatting with the urinal all alone in the bathroom,
Moved away from home yet not grown,

That was a thought stuck in the mind of a lost and confused Soul,
Who may feel used because of his mental scars and bruised ego,

Interrupted thoughts, mind splitting like exploding stainless steel vaults,
Causing a quake of the earth,
Resembling the mother's womb upon the shaking of birth,

Rose to be independent as a descendant of excellence,
Taking my time to reach the top, developing patience,
For my Soul is a virtue of my God and my thoughts Greatness.

Closing Walls

I am trying to run away mentally,
Because I am stuck physically,
Spiritually, running, ducking, and dodging
Everything on the trail of me,

The walls are closing in…

Liquor singing in my veins,
Chronic bronchitis dancing in my lungs
Flowing through my blood from the weed in my brain…
About 6 more feet to climb, but the thoughts in my mind won't let me go…

The Walls are closing in,
I feel as if my feet were super glued to the floor,
The Walls are closing,
Like stage fright with no show in-store,

The Walls are closing in,

While in the past I could get out of trouble with a sinly grin,
I can't believe the walls are closing in…
They're closing, they're closing…The walls are closing in…

I was once a witness to an artist going through the

Sh-Klak-Klak, Sh-Klak-Klak,
But now the Sh-Klak-Klak has happened to Random
Thought again,

Damn all of my torture,
All of my pain, the extent of my sadness,
Are the results of my sins again.

Check Out Time

With Him, you must communicate to participate,
You must pray in order to keep it straight,
You have to manipulate to elevate and don't discriminate,
But anticipate the opening and closing of heavens gate,

Don't be the Devil's bait, no time to hesitate,
You must emancipate yourself to dictate the state of your own fate,
So check the date before it's to late,
It's almost check out time.

Welcome To My World

Welcome, welcome to all comers, come in…visit with me inside of my mentality, walk and hold my hand, as we stroll beneath the darkness of the sun, be the psycho-lunatic pappy of my son,
…Welcome to my world…

Dance with the shadows of my Soul, be the judging poet of my Soul, then tell me my thoughts,
Can society understand the mind of a kind-hearted man whose only desire is to kill others with kindness, even though I live in a mental darkness?
…Welcome to my World…

I suffer from pains in my brains, I don't know what it is, but there is something funny in my veins, my energy drained, my flesh shaking from being insane, death creates fertilization for the grain of the wheat we eat, you know healthy shit to make home cooked meals, wishing I could swim away like seals, but I can't because I'm locked in a mental cage, within me is hostility, whom is the trigger of my mental rage, because I am an entertainer I escape from my cage when my presence graces the stage, smiling with a hidden rage, my eyes appearing strange, like a white flame, realizing life is not a game,

I am lucky to be alive, and I'm not ashamed to cry for the pain I cause because of my own lie, I show love to all but some say I'm selfish, because I don't care if I live or die, skidding on wet pavement, mentally yelling like...
Cavemen...
Feeling like a lost sperm in...
Semen...
With my Mind, Body, and Soul imprisoned six feet beneath a cemented pavement...

Welcome to my World.

Eternity

The start of a new beginning, no more sinning,
People grinning, Picked apart by their heartless intension,
Unknown words mentioned with much anticipation,
No hesitation to be part of a great creation, a magical sensation,

On a day of fate, no ending date at the drop of a dime no stopping time,
With the opportunity to elevate above the harsh state of a virtual reality,
Approaching insanity, insane principality,
Un-chosen ability, the ability to pray, heard by a friend,
Eternity is forever there is no end.

Thugged Out

Thugged out is being locked up in the mind,
Creating imprisonment of your dreams,
Causing outrageous outbursts of words and
behaviors never seen,

To live thugged out is a waste of time, brothers
killing brothers, sisters killing babies,
Babies killing mothers, lovers killing themselves,
Leaving their significant others alone on earth
beneath the clouds cover,

To live thugged out is not as hard as it may seem,
Just imprison your thoughts live your nightmares
and throw away your dreams.

Craziness

How could you lay with a woman?
Maybe create a woman,
Then leave because of your laziness,
That's just craziness…

Why can't you just be a man?
To raise a man, my brother you made a man,
Then leave because of your tiredness,
That's just craziness…

Who told you to hump the girl?
If you didn't love the girl,
And disguise it with your loveliness,
That's just craziness…

When do you see your child?
Do you even love your child?
Did you forget you had a child, is it forgetfulness?
That's just craziness…

So you accidentally hit a lady,
How could you mistreat a lady,
Then say it was your angriness,
That's just craziness…

What kind of things do you do for your wife?

Besides beat, cheat, freak, and then leave your wife,
I think it is unmanliness…
That's just craziness…

Before you think about going home,
You better make sure you have a home,
Home is pure and full of joyfulness,
Yet your heart is filled with nothing but craziness…

At home a mother and her child need love and support,
But because of your craziness they will happily receive your checks,
Signed child Support…

I Am

I am the dirt within me is the wind,
Through my eyes you can see flowing rivers,
when the water raises you can sense my pain,

I am he and he is me, He is my power, He gave me my Soul,
I am an image of his imagination,
A great sensation he has given me his power to glow,

I am light, I am day, I am dark, I am night,
He revives my might upon the words I pray,
Reassuring my eye sight, no longer in fright,
Because I am brave,

Just like my enslaved ancestors to be free is what I crave,
I will never achieve freedom if I continue with this mental rage,
They tried to destroy us because the devil could not put shackles on our brains,
I am a descendant of greatness, within me is a legend;
I can feel it in my veins.

Rate

Rate the stats that are proven facts,
Facts that back the information stacks of life on the tracks,
From blacks to whites,
N-Words don't see the light,

A Black man has the sight and the power to shine brighter than the suns fire,
Saying hire the liar,
Then blame the buyer on the wirer
For labeling the worker the slave,
My people are brave because we crave to be the best and oversee the rest,
Soon to do away with the need for a bullet proof vest,

We conquer our stress by praying on our knees with our chin tucked to our chest,
We passed the test of time physically and by the strength of our minds this is now our time to divide my ancestral past by the turning of time.

(Knowledge + Love – Hate) = Freedom

Not my name

My Brother:
You are my brother, you are strong, you are intelligent, and you are loved. The name you carry, you are blessed with. You have never been anyone's N-word, not now, not tomorrow, not ever! You are destined for greatness so with pride you state your claim. Neglect the ignorance of disrespect, stand your ground,
Speak Up, Speak Out… Shout if you have to!
That is not my name!

My Sister:
You are my sister, you are my brother's strength, you are beautiful and you are loved. You are a Queen with pride and virtue. Have you been labeled as a slut, tramp, whore, skeezer, or have been victim of some prostituted money hungry sex pleaser; being called any name that is of derogatory meaning; Lift your eyes unto glory, stand strong and say that name does not belong to me. Tell them you are not a hoe; you do not answer to bitch. Rebuke their ignorance which surely is a shame.
Speak Up, Speak Out… Shout if you have to!
That is not my name!

Name Me a Hurricane

We were floating in an ocean of misery, as the hull of
the ship danced across a grave of history.
Death in the zillions lay beneath us,
My ancestors, their ancestors, bodies and trapped
Souls of those that came before us lay beneath us,

We've been taken from our homelands to do the
work for these indecent beings,
They kidnapped our Kings out of our Kingdoms,
forced to speak their language and eat their tasteless
food, No one knows our names or our family history
because to all of those ignorant of reality we don't
exist,

I know other wise because the Souls of the lost are
speaking through Random Thought, saying, "Allow
yourself to rearrange your thought process, dance to
the rhythm of the love drum in your chest,"

Random Thought has been chosen to interpret not
another language but given the ability to hear and
understand the voice of the lost and forgotten,
My Soul not haunted but uplifted with Pride to
recognize what is all around me, realizing my
destiny as I think and write attempting to escape and
allow the world to feel all of me,

Chained to another, alive and breathing fine, but
because they took the life of a friend of mine, as they
tossed him over the side, not caring if we are
shackled together, not only did they take his life,
But they took mine,

Now I walk around the deep dark 7-seas,
When I connect with the right Soul to listen to me,
I'll provide you a song to sing,
Listen as I yell from misty waters to populated lands,
When I cry out the hurricane that shall be named
after me,

Hello my name is Katrina... nice to meet you.

Elevation

Raised to inspire, never taught to be a liar,
But to soar higher than the average man,
You know do whatever… I desire because I can,

As a man with my life in God's hands for I am a descendant of greatness, I have developed patience thru my inheritance, I show acceptance to all who understands this, never getting upset because my Queen is from whom I get kissed, No longer rolling over and shedding a tear for this as I live out loud, no longer in silence,

Elevation… I am this…
Penetration I do this…
Perspiration, you sweat this…
Without hesitation you love this…
Whether you show up or not; I am a performer, I shall still read this, so peep this, don't miss this, this isn't the time forget this,

I am the Soul of the New Age Lyricist,
The elevator of elevation so elevate your mind before you run out of Time or your life will be like this rhyme…**OVER.**

More Than a Random Thought

I am a Random Thought, I…am….a…..Random Thought…..yet at times I do Random Things, I even have random dreams,

Dreams of nothingness and useless meanings, yet always remembering the voice that said, "I Had A Dream" encouraging me to ignite the stage lights in my mind to do maintenance checks on my life preparing to take flight on another level of this thing we call life,

Preparing to live beyond my dreams, as I educate the little black boys, little white girls, little white boys, and little black girls that I have been chosen to raise may benefit from the ideologies Dr. King's Dream,

As hard as it may seem, we have the power to control our dreams,
Today it is up us to believe and…Continue the Dream…
Share the goodness and knowledge we were taught…
Through Christ and the reality of a dream,
I shall be more than just a Random Thought.

What is my Name?

Pure unprovoked properly guided by innocence, once the true face of our children

Misinformed by the provocations of ignorance and false visions of reality

Diluted messages of what's right and amplified proclamations of wrong doing

Uneducated hypothesis with thesis statements more ignorant than those who simply don't know

Supported by fantasies of independent hustlers after money, cars, clothes and even video games

Played by characters wearing gang colors in political disguise yet
Neglecting gang rules and policies, Allow Me to Introduce Myself…

Hello, my name is CONGRESS.

GIVE ME FREEDOM

For Centuries they have abused, degraded, and shamed me into shaming myself
With their guns they have forced my fathers into singing their rhythm-less songs and eat the scraps of their tasteless food,
They have beat fear into my mothers influencing them to turn away from their kings and neglect the responsibility of their love for me
Eradicating their memories of how they are direct blood lines of kings and queens
Who lived a life with no shackles & cuffs, they were free.

Free from the ignorance of human captivity with shackles of the past haunting my present and poisoning my future with images of cuffs and jail cells, well with me this doesn't sit well because my mind is like a bottomless wishing well foretelling my resurrection to greatness, our success will lead to their madness and reckless thoughts
Give me Freedom, No more Shackles & Cuffs

My son, Today
I will no not call him Master, he will Give me my FREEDOM, or I'll take it! The Lord as my witness, I will be free, No more Shackles, No more Cuffs, Free to be me, free to love my children, and free to love my Queen... My son, remember this day there is something special about June 19th.

Unhand my child, I will bite my tongue no more, no longer will you divide my village, mistreat and disrespect my family
To your dislike and curiosity, I've heard the news I know the soldiers are coming
I can hear the swag, and smooth rhythm of their marching, the cadence calling out to me
I'm feeling spiritually lifted, by way of Jesus Christ it is God that Strengthens me

Proverbs 3:35 says that "The wise shall inherit glory: but shame shall be the promotions of fools." For all of you whom thought my people to be fools, witness the shine of our glory as we come up from the valley of very dry bones to return home and to live again

Witness the songs of the village as our Kings and Queens sing to our children and teach them to love and smile again. Wait… Wait…Wait…
I can hear drums… I can hear the sound of them marching and singing old Negro spirituals again… The Cadence is calling my name… I shall never call you master again… My son, we will be free again. Trust me now, I believe in my soul, Freedom is coming… we will be free again…

Then the soldier said to me, "Brothers and Sisters, two and one half year hath past, and your freedom has been granted, in effect since the 1st day of the year in 1863 you have been free."

Today is a new beginning, starting with the ending of slavery; with you as the employer and myself the paid employee. Now, we will not stop here, my son will learn and grow strong, his life to far exceed the life of me. The day will come where we will celebrate this day, as our own bosses and you will work for someone that looks like me, yet we will not stoop as low as you, for you will be treated as a human being so that your children can grow with a sense of dignity.

I will no not call you Master, you will Give me my FREEDOM, The Lord as my witness, I will be free, No more Shackles, No more Cuffs, Free to be me, free to love my children, and free to love my Queen… Today we Celebrate Juneteenth!

Today WE ARE FREE!

Continue the Dream

I am a product of Dr. King. I can feel the inheritance of his voice. To be one of the "little black boys", in his dreams… is my destiny, and my choice. Could you imagine yourself dreaming his dream, nonetheless walking in his shoes…The time is now to Continue his Dream, which path shall you choose?

Will you be that N-word, accepting some crazed virtual reality that says you are meant to be nothing more than the ignorance of that adjective that some fools use as nouns and verbs …Or, will you be that brother and sister that brings the strength of a dream into reality, continue Dr. King's Dream and conquer our Nations Insanity for racial equality…

Because…

The insanity is killing me, literally, look behind these bars, dream about the grave, death to violence, look at that mother's favorite picture on the right, yes sir; the photo of her once little bundle of joy, playing with his/her toys, with a smile like mine, and skin like yours…

Sh-Klak-Klak….Boom…!!!!!
There goes a shot in the air!

Can't you see?
There goes a shot in the air!!!!

Why are you just standing there, run to safety live for me, you know that those whom are ignorant don't care about you and damn sure don't care about me. I have the strength of a million men marching, proving with God on my side, I'll never die… my brother, my sister, Help save a life to change life, start by changing their mind…don't let this dream die … help me save the second coming of we…The Time is Now!... I choose to…Continue the Dream…

…Because…

I am a product of Dr. King. I can feel the inheritance of his voice. To be one of the "little black boys", in his dreams… is my destiny, and my choice. Could you imagine yourself dreaming his dream, nonetheless walking in his shoes…The time is now to Continue his Dream, which path shall you choose?

To be a slave to your own mind… or will you be Free at last, free at last, thank God almighty…

WE ARE FREE LAST!

I Cry for my People

Sister, I know you are all cried out, I can see the pain in
your eyes, Confused and hurt resulting in self-doubt
You have been spiritually broken, now Only God can hear
your cries, In your mind you have seen too much and
cried too many times, From here on out you have to decide
to never cry… although, you are dying inside…

My Brother, I sense your pain has turned into anger
Because of your fear, you even greet those that you know
as if they are strangers, As you feel as if you are in a
strange land, doing a strangers will, Not acknowledging
that you have become a stranger to yourself Clouding
your judgment, and being confused about what's really
real. In your mind you have seen too much and cried too
many times
From here on out you have to decide to never cry…
although, you are dying inside…

My People, I am sad to be witness to the limp in your walk
Through me, you can talk freely and openly about your
joys and your fears, Think of me, as your Random
Thought…

You have been emotionally shattered by the yelling and
shouting, frustrated at the lack ability to simply share

good memories of childhood years, In your mind you have seen too much and cried too many times
From here on out you have to decide to never cry... although, you are dying inside...

You are all cried out externally, leaving you surrounded by your invisible tears, God sent me here for you, find comfort in my arms; Witness my tears cry for you, And you'll see my tears are not mine, I hurt, I laugh, and I smile for my people. In your mind you have seen too much and cried too many times, From here on out you have to decide to never cry... although, you are dying inside...

My life has been redefined, In God I have the strength of the heavens above, I have been blessed with the gift of crying for my people. I want you to know, that each one of you, are loved In your mind you have seen too much and cried too many times From here on out you have to decide to never cry... although, you are dying inside...

So, rest yourself now; let me cry for you... plus me... plus you... multiplied by us... one million times. I want you to smile; it is I that will Cry for my People.

Sounds of the Village

Laughter, glorified shouting, singing, and the sounds of feet dancing

Feet dancing happily to melodic tunes while working to build love based off of fairy tale stories of yesterday

Yesterday filled with the strength and images of Kings & Queens maintaining magnificent empires

SPEAK UP!

Empires of complete families with united sons & daughters, with loving mothers & Fathers present as King

King is the man that was the minister of the household as the protector & provider

Provider of stability, security, food, emotional wealth and love for his Queen

SPEAK UP!

Queen also known as the mother of civilization and the young's first teacher

Teacher, teaching around camp fires using stones, sticks, and stars to educate the children about life

Life being more than just worrying about me, myself, and I... because...

SPEAK UP!

I have to learn from the ideals and experiences of yesterday, so that I can pave a road today, to ensure you have a road to travel for tomorrow.

Tomorrow you will travel a road paved with faith from the Sounds of love within the villages of yesterday.

Yesterday did not begin with Slavery and disconnect between people.

SPEAK UP!

People, we are the people of today planning for a better tomorrow full of optimism and opportunity

Opportunity for your success awaits you. Believe in yourself and respect the work of yesterday, to enhance your understanding today.

Today, free your mind, dance with praise for the wonders of the Creator, and dream of the sounds of the village so that you may have strength to lead the way into tomorrow.

Sounds of the Village

The Negro Speaking of Rivers

I'm the Negro speaking of rivers, speaking real talk, truth, keeping it 100 and making you shiver, from my yell to my whisper... now SPEAK UP! Then SPEAK OUT! If you hear me, Blink twice if you see me, right foot stomp... 2 times, do the cha-cha slide if you feel me, You see I'm the negro speaking of rivers, although times have changed, the direction of the current in which the river flows, stays the same.

My soul has grown deep like oceans traveling across ancient lands that up until now have only existed in my virtual reality, I've known dry valleys, so I'm learning from Langston trying to fill my intellectual cup so that I can drink knowledge up and breathe my virtual into a physical existence... screaming viva la resistance as I fight with mighty insistence to prevent my own people from eradicating the African existence within us....

I'm the Negro speaking of rivers, speaking real talk, truth; keeping it 100 and making you shiver, from my yell to my whisper... now SPEAK UP! Then SPEAK OUT! If you hear me, Blink twice if you see me, right foot stomp... 2 times, do the cha-cha slide if you feel me, You see I'm the negro speaking of rivers, although times have changed, the direction of the current in which the river flows, stays the same.

From being sold down the Mississippi, to being beat, killed, and destroyed by images of myself being sold by me… psychological weaknesses within me leading to a self-inflicted slave mentality… I am not your Nigga!

I'm the man that stands before you singing *"Weary Blues"* like Bro. Hughes, Searching for A Gift to Sing, while James Weldon and J. Rosamond Johnson sing an anthem about Lifting Every Voice, Educating the young men on the river banks about how slavery in the past was a thing of circumstance… today it's a choice

I'm the Negro speaking of rivers, speaking real talk, truth, keeping it 100 and making you shiver, from my yell to my whisper… now SPEAK UP! Then SPEAK OUT! If you hear me, Blink twice if you see me, right foot stomp… 2 times, do the cha-cha slide if you feel me, You see I'm the negro speaking of rivers, although times have changed, the direction of the current in which the river flows, stays the same.

We've gone from playing "catch-a-girl, get-a-girl" to playing songs like "I kissed a girl", instead crooning to the Temptations singing ballads about "My Girl"… We've gone from little boys playing with toys to finding out that the nice young "lady" in skinny jeans and a pony tail is really a boy… Now I'm not judging, so don't get it twisted, we've gone from the pursuit of happiness to constant implications of sadness, a world full of madness and those lying bastards at the "head of state" could care less about this.

They could care less about the people that are dying from the drugs they are trying, because every time the "law" bust up a purchase they put the drugs back on the street to be purchased by the highest nigga, my bad I must be tripping I meant by the highest bidder, although the dilemma of drugs is an every race situation,

I'm talking about the money made from attempting to keep the poor in poverty and destruction of the sounds of unity that once existed in the open within the African nation… Encouraging the violence and diluting messages about fighting the power, by putting the guns on the street for the inner city youth to use for murder and be talked about on the news during the 6 o'clock hour, Still they can't destroy us, our Strength flows like rivers.

I'm the Negro speaking of rivers, speaking real talk, truth; keeping it 100 and making you shiver, from my yell to my whisper… now SPEAK UP! Then SPEAK OUT! If you hear me, Blink twice if you see me, right foot stomp… 2 times, do the cha-cha slide if you feel me, You see I'm the negro speaking of rivers, although times have changed, the direction of the current in which the river flows, stays the same.

I'm speaking about the silliness of sagging pants and the destruction caused by different colored rags, from gang related issues to the grind of independent hustlers, ignorant of the penalties awarded for senseless crimes, because in their mind they're just trying to survive, the harshness of their inherited reality existing in an atmosphere of little positivity and a lack of inspiration to spark the least bit of motivation to work for something better than what they're after… instead they're dying at the river banks with a legacy that influences pain, grief, and anger.

Although our youth are in danger traveling overflowing rivers filled with commotion, it's not too late to change a life and see our youth live to their full potential with hopes to see the mouth of the river, drink from the benefits of the ocean.

I'm the Negro speaking of rivers, speaking real talk, truth; keeping it 100 and making you shiver, from my yell to my whisper… now SPEAK UP! Then SPEAK OUT! If you hear me, Blink twice if you see me, right foot stomp… 2 times, do the cha-cha slide if you feel me, You see I'm the negro speaking of rivers, although times have changed, the direction of the current in which the river flows, stays the same.

State of Emergency

I can no longer stand by and watch images of me being destroyed by ignorance and "I don't care" attitudes. We have fought too long and come too far to be set back by US. Set back by a self-inflicted slave mentality and destruction of the man in the mirror by the man who stands there. Today I stand on the shoulders of giants, breathing heavy with war paint covering my soul… I am here to fight the good fight and save our children. We must save our children from stereotypes and society placed stigmas that our children carry with them into their futures, which in the end stunt their growth and cut their futures short.

I declare today a State of Emergency

My Last Breath

With My last breath I pray My fingers are able to stroke my keyboard like 8th notes on a piano striking tunes to a masterpiece of lyrically induced melodies and rhythms of knowledge beating down the walls of ignorance with snare drums bringing the ratta-tat-tat while the bass drum of my voice brings the boom and the timpani of my words join together manifesting scores for percussionist inspired persuasions of HIP-HOP… I'll keep spitting poet-Ucation until my last breath stops.

MY Last Poem

This is my last poem, the last rhythmic verse to ever spill from my random thoughts
No more spoken word grooves, love stories, or day dream writing… it will be locked away in my psychological vaults
Creativity excommunicated from reality, this is merely an individual decision to be charged to no one else's faults.

This is my Last Poem

No more screaming sha-klack-klack, and no more black revolutionary folk tales
No more speaking up in the park, open mics, no more nothing… everything now derailed
No more Poet-Ucation, no more speaking out, no more shouting, even if I have to, it was never about book sales

This is my Last Poem

I will no longer write and allow my thoughts to flow thru my pen to do my talking for me
There will be no more melodic tunes and dancing moves, nor talks of a gorgeous "she"
I'm done feeling the beat, I no longer care about that walk, or becoming the dance of a melody

This is my Last Poem

Writing poetry is now oblivious to me, and I refuse to slow
down nonetheless look back
I refuse to write another poetic verse or record my voice
upon another musical track
Those that were made uncomfortable can rest and be
easy… I'm stepping black

This is my Last Poem

And I have committed to no longer writing poetic verse or
implications of symbolic meanings
No more inspirational words, no one has to worry about
any disrespectful sayings
The show has been cancelled, I will do any more features,
and not accepting any more poetic meetings

This is my Last Poem

I'm done speaking in parables, metaphors and similes will
no further occupy my time
I'm done making up stories and speaking the truth will
only be speaking in the far ends of my mind
This is my last poem, so whatever else that may spill out
into this world is not guaranteed to rhyme

This is my Last Poem

Please visit our website:
www.rennellparker.com

Social Networks
www.facebook.com/rennell.parker
www.linkedin.com/in/rennellparker
www.twitter.com/renpin

www.ingramcontent.com/pod-product-compliance
Lightning Source LLC
Chambersburg PA
CBHW032135040426
42449CB00005B/250